# THE INTIMACY GURU

*Helping Modern Couples Reignite Passion, Pleasure, and Connection in Their Relationships*

ANGIE D. LEE

Author of
*Discovering Lita & Something New*

Copyright © 2023 by Angie D. Lee

All rights reserved. No part of this book may be reproduced or used in any manner without written permission of the copyright owner except for the use of quotations in a book review. For more information, address: angie@angiedlee.com.

ISBN 978-1-7328641-4-6 (paperback)

www.angiedlee.com

*To every couple who seeks to explore
the depths of their relationship with love*

# Contents

Introduction .................................................................... vii

I. **All of Me: Receiving and Expressing Intimacy In Your Relationship** ........................................... 1
   1. Can You Handle The Truth? ........................... 7
   2. Set Aside Your Pride .................................... 11
   3. Closer Than Close ....................................... 13

II. **When It Hurts: Resolving Conflict With Love** ...... 15
   1. The Three Ts: Timing, Tone, & Tact ............... 17
   2. I Have Something To Say ............................. 19
   3. Effective Conflict Resolution ....................... 21

III. **The Spice of Life: Strengthening Your Physical Intimacy & Sexual Passion** ............................... 23
   1. Are You Living or Just Existing? .................. 25
   2. Indulge the Senses ..................................... 29
   3. Become a Student of Your Partner .............. 33

   *Notes* ....................................................... 37
   *Credits* .................................................... 41

# Introduction

*"Children must be taught how to think, not what to think."*

MARGARET MEAD
American Cultural Anthropologist

*"The way we talk to our children becomes their inner voice."*

PEGGY O'MARA
Author, Editor and Publisher of
Mothering Magazine from 1980-2011

I believe the first time I conceptualized intimacy was when I was about six or seven years old. My grandmother would always say that I was an observer and not much of a talker, which is kind of ironic considering I'm a public speaker and I talk to people for a living as an intimacy coach. My grandmother's recount of my behaviors during childhood and adolescence is one that I truly cherish because I was considered a quiet child and less outspoken in comparison to my sister and cousins. This caused me to feel a bit overlooked at times, but my grandmother pointed out to me that I was just alert and watchful and that there was nothing wrong with that.

I loved that explanation because I felt like my grandmother really understood me at that moment. As a child, I'd been mistaken for shy and maybe even a bit timid in certain situations, which felt more like criticism than a compliment. But then, I would think about what my grandmother said and that would help me to feel embraced for who I was.

I was always curious and quite fascinated with people in general, often allowing me to sit back and watch them. I paid attention to what people would say and how they would say it, but I also paid attention to their actions. I became intrigued with why people said one thing but did another. Being so observant helped me to really understand my environment and honestly, to ensure my safety.

If there were times my words were few and I was staring off somewhere, my grandmother would often ask, *"What's on your mind, Lady?"* That was her way of connecting with me; trying to understand my world as it was playing out in my head. It didn't seem like a huge deal then, but I absolutely love it now when people ask me what I'm thinking about and how something makes me feel. It reminds me of my grandmother's desire to just understand me and not make assumptions about me. I felt accepted.

For a moment, I want you to take a trip down memory lane of your childhood. You will more than likely be able to discover your first experiences with intimacy as well, whether positive or negative. Then, I want you to travel back to the present moment and ask yourself if your upbringing plays a significant role in how you relate to your partner today.

When a person feels validated, this tends to diffuse tension and even feelings of isolation or lack of support. When partners dismiss each other's ideas, thoughts, or feelings and automatically make conclusions about each other without seeking to understand, this tends to diminish the intimacy between them. Typically when this occurs, closeness begins to fade.

True intimacy allows people to feel seen, heard, and understood. When these components of a relationship are present, closeness tends to develop. You can also sustain that closeness the more you become intentional about cultivating it. In this book, I want to help you and your partner regain that connection by being able to receive and give intimacy in your relationship, resolve conflict with love, and strengthen your physical intimacy and sexual passion as well.

Remember, the more you seek to understand one another creates empathy between the two of you and a willingness to explore the depths of one another. This is what keeps the spark alive in your relationship and a desire for more.

ALL OF ME

# Receiving and Expressing Intimacy In Your Relationship

---

*"There's so much intimacy in understanding. Someone who doesn't understand you is not going to know how to love you, because they don't know who you are."*

ANONYMOUS

*"I define connection as the energy that exists between people when they feel seen, heard, and valued; when they can give and receive without judgment; and when they derive sustenance and strength from the relationship."*

BRENÉ BROWN
American Professor, Author, and Podcast Host

Isn't it interesting that sharing our innermost thoughts and feelings with someone can feel scarier than the thought of climbing Mount Kilimanjaro? Why is that? Well, in many instances, vulnerability can feel like a weakness instead of strength. When we allow ourselves to be vulnerable, we basically position ourselves to be judged. Judgment tends to lead to guilt and shame and in many instances, it can feel like someone has the upper hand and can take advantage of us. Now based on that analysis, who in their right mind would want to be vulnerable?

Here's the thing. Vulnerability allows for people to understand each other on a deeper level, including their insecurities and their deepest feelings, which can lead to greater empathy in both partners[1]. Vulnerability is the driving force of connection and we close ourselves off to the endless possibilities in our relationships when we do not allow ourselves to be open in this way.

In the past fifty plus years or so, I believe we've received sort of mixed messages as it pertains to vulnerability. We seemed closer and more connected as a society in the sense that we experienced more in-person interaction. We engaged in frequent family dinners, children connected with each other sans digital devices, and we marched hand in hand for various causes and initiatives. Now on the flip side, we were also encouraged to sweep things under the rug, keep private business "in the house or in the family", we turned a blind eye to situations that may have placed us in precarious situations, and even died with a boatload of secrets because many times vulnerability was seen as a weakness or even more extreme; may have gotten us killed.

No wonder receiving and expressing vulnerability can feel like such a frightening task and also downright confusing. A person may wonder if they are really safe sharing their truth, even in their most intimate relationships. So basically, will you feel safe enough to express to your partner that your father used to tiptoe in your room at night as a child and touch you in unwanted places? If not, this may be a huge reason why you've built a proverbial wall which makes physical intimacy a challenge in your relationship. Or, are you nervous about expressing that you tend to experience some form of social anxiety because you were bullied or teased significantly as a child? Or, you may even be uncomfortable sharing that you're always trying to be the "fixer" or overachiever in your relationship because as a child, you felt the only time you were noticed was when you completed tasks with flying colors or catered to someone else's needs while neglecting your own.

Yes, we're going to go a tad bit deep here for a second so I understand if this starts to make you feel a little uneasy. But just know that I'm not going to leave you with an open wound. We're also going to discuss some strategies with regards to helping you become more vulnerable with your partner in addition to being able to receive their truth as well.

In the introduction of this book, I shared an experience I personally had as a child which still remains a positive one that has shaped me significantly as it pertains to intimacy. But, I've also had experiences that didn't quite feel so good and later on became an issue that I had to work through for the benefit of my intimate relationships.

Growing up, my parents were legally married but did not always reside in the same home and were not "connected" in a lot of ways. Being the observant child I was, I saw things and in my child-like mind I tried to make sense of what was taking place. I grew up in the 80s so that should tell you all you need to know about what that time was like; basically not questioning your parents. Even if you felt you were well within your rights to confront them about something, you were scolded because you were expected to "stay in a child's place" and the double whammy was little girls were expected to be "seen and not heard". When you read these phrases, does not that resonate with you? Does it bring back some not so good memories? Does it make you feel like your voice was sometimes stifled as a child? It's okay, you're not going to get into trouble if you admit these things. We're learning how to be vulnerable, remember? And, this is also a safe space.

Now the question is, how did this play out in my intimate relationships? Well, I'm glad you asked. It became a learned behavior that when I had something on my mind or had questions about things that confused me, caused me sadness, or even anger, my initial reaction was to not say anything. I sat with those feelings quite often by myself for fear of judgment, ridicule, or even punishment. I also grew up in a very religious family where the standards and stakes were even higher. Thankfully, my mom was a school teacher (early childhood to be exact) who understood child development so she was very aware and in tune with my sister and me. She knew how to address things with us without making us feel like we had no voice. She allowed us to ask questions (within reason, of course; this was still the 80s, remember?), share our feelings with her, and she saved space for all of the emotions we experienced that came along with growing up in a broken home. She was and still is literally an angel on earth. But my mother was also dealing with not being as vulnerable as she would have liked because even though my parents' marriage appeared strained most days, the community of people in her life, which were her church family, just told her to "pray about it". So she had no one to really confide in, thus leading to feelings of isolation.

This now becomes cyclical. Yes, my mom, sister, and I were close and we would share things amongst the three of us, but I didn't always feel that closeness with my dad. Now as an adult, I can make sense of things a bit better regarding his personal journey. But in his absence, and many times with no explanation as to what was happening between him and my mom, I did not feel reassured by him, nor did I feel seen or protected by him.

I distinctly remember one time I drummed up enough courage to ask my dad about his whereabouts and why he was not consistently present in our lives. I was only twelve years old at the time but I was fed up and I was tired of acting as if we were a solid family just to save face for others. I practiced saying what I wanted to say to him so that when the words finally escaped my lips and traveled to his ears, I would hopefully receive some kind of explanation or understanding for all of the years of confusion and having to stay quiet for so long in order to not bring any embarrassment or shame to our family. So I took the chance at being vulnerable with my feelings. Well, let's just say that didn't go over too well. My dad's response was dismissive and honestly, quite cold. This is when my proverbial wall went up and I thought to myself, *"if my own dad can shut me down in this way as if I was just a random person he was talking to on the street, then I refuse to allow anyone else into that space again."*

Since then, I'd always been comfortable with receiving the truth of others because I knew how it felt to have my feelings invalidated and dismissed. But the alternative part of me wouldn't allow myself to bare my soul to communicate to others because I'd always been hanging onto that twelve year old girl who was just looking to be seen, heard, and validated by her daddy. I didn't want to experience that feeling again so I muted that side of myself. Little did I know, it would have an impact on my relationships; more specifically with my husband.

Family is the primary agent of socialization during childhood and, even in adolescence, it continues to be more influential than any other single factor[2]. Over time, experiences in the family of origin, particularly the quality of the parent-child relationship, have a major impact upon subsequent patterns of interaction with adult romantic partners through their impact on youth's acquisition of characteristics important to intimate relationship success[3]. This is one of the reasons why it's extremely important to explore your childhood and adolescent experiences anytime you're having challenges with vulnerability in your relationships. I often tell my clients this is where many of the answers can be found if you're willing to do the work.

## Let's Unpack:

1. What was your relationship like with your parents? Was it close-knit? Strained? Distant? Volatile? A hybrid of various things?

2. Did you feel seen and heard? Did you feel like you had a voice? Could you share your deepest, darkest thoughts? Did you feel included in family matters or were you expected to just follow the rules?

3. What was your family's view of you? Were you the performer? The fixer? The scapegoat? The blacksheep? The successful one? The failure?

What you will find when you answer these questions is a bit of a blueprint as to how you "show up" in your marriage or relationship. These are the areas within yourself you have to be cognizant of when seeking to be vulnerable with your partner. In order for them to be able to accept who you truly are, you have to be willing to go a bit deeper and be honest with yourself about all of the facets of your life. Like I mentioned earlier, Mount Kilimanjaro, my friends. But the benefits of that level of vulnerability can reap huge benefits.

# Can You Handle The Truth?

This is where vulnerability can become a bit tricky. So we've already mentioned that it can be a scary thing, right? But what's even scarier is when our partners are actually vulnerable with us and we can't handle it. I'll give you an example. Say for instance your partner comes home from work and he shares his consistent frustrations with you about upper management overlooking his contributions to the business. He tells you that they even had the nerve to promote the new guy on the job with less experience because of nepotism. Your partner reaches out for a hug and you sort of push him away because he hasn't taken out the trash in the past week and it's piling up so you begin to scold him.

Your partner becomes frustrated with you and calls you selfish and careless. Now you're both at each other's throats and your partner yells, "I'm sick of this _____!" You can add whatever choice words you'd like in that space. He further proceeds to say, "all I ask for is a little comfort every now and then and maybe even some recognition for the things I do right wouldn't hurt either." Now, of course, this may feel like an attack on you from your partner, but within his anger, your partner is expressing vulnerability. It's not exactly the most ideal way for him to share his feelings but nonetheless, he is exposing *his* truth. It may not be *your* truth, but it's how *he* feels.

With my empathic and therapeutic ear, I hear that he wants some form of intimacy, whether it be physical and/or emotional by him saying, "all I ask for is a little comfort every now and then." And then I hear that he may be seeking some form of validation or affirmation when he says, "and maybe even some recognition for the things I do right wouldn't hurt either."

With regards to this scenario, we're going to say that this is a generally healthy relationship free from major toxicity, but clearly both partners are triggered and it's being expressed in this way.

So, let's rewind this story for a minute. Your partner now comes in from work and makes the same statement about his job. This time, you either reach for him or ask him sincerely, "would you like for me to hold you?", his response would either be "yes" or he may just fall into your arms from the weight of everything he's been experiencing at work. He may have really needed that because physical touch may be his primary love language. You may even state to him while he's holding you, "Babe, I think you're amazing at what you do. It's unfortunate they don't see what I see. Maybe we can talk later about some ways that may assist you with continuously working in such an environment or maybe even exploring other job opportunities. Whatever you decide, I support you."

Your response has now affirmed him and you've even thrown in some quality time because your focus is on your connection during the present moment as opposed to being distracted with other tasks or things that have nothing to do with the situation at hand. Now, I know what you're thinking, but what about the garbage that needs to be taken out and all of the other things I've asked him to do that he doesn't follow through with? See, I knew that's where you were headed, but we'll address how to handle conflict effectively and with love in the next chapter. Right now, we're focusing more on receiving and expressing intimacy.

Due to you allowing your partner to share the intimate details of his job and how it's been affecting him, you've created a space for him to feel safe which can encourage him to be even more vulnerable with you. But let's say that you *have* been allowing him to be vulnerable with you, but he constantly "needs" you in ways that feel like it's draining you emotionally. Perhaps you've both agreed to attend counseling to address an ongoing conflict because of your partner's need to be consistently affirmed or him not feeling satisfied in your relationship unless he's receiving physical touch from you all the time.

You have your first session with a couples counselor and it is revealed by your partner that he was often referred to as the underachiever in his family when he was growing up. He also reflects upon his family treating him with disdain because they felt he wasn't good enough. Your partner admits that he was always reprimanded for his mistakes, but never acknowledged for his accomplishments. He also mentioned that his family wasn't exactly loving in their approach. They rarely hugged each other or said "I love you" and the counselor concludes that this is probably one of the reasons your partner desires heavy doses of affirmation and physical intimacy.

Can you handle your partner's truth or do you start feeling like this is too much to take on? Do you find yourself throwing your partner's vulnerability back in his face when he upsets you? Do you now see your partner's vulnerability as a weakness as opposed to a strength?

If you've been in a relationship where your partner exposes his or her truth to you, are you able to handle it or do you find yourself blaming your partner for how their truth makes you feel? These are tough questions for sure, but they must be answered in order to build a stronger connection with your partner.

So, how do you receive your partner's truth? It first begins with accepting yours. When you can accept certain areas about yourself and be willing to expose them to your partner, you can begin to embrace your partner's truth as well. This is what I mean by being able to handle their truth. It doesn't mean that it's always comfortable or something you agree with, but you can allow your partner to be transparent with you about their wants and needs while working towards connectedness.

## Tips for handling your partner's truth:

1. **Check your reaction.** How you react to your partner's truth says a lot about how it resonates with you. Ask yourself, "why does my partner's truth affect me the way that it does?" Sit with that answer for a while before responding.

2. **Empathize.** Try not to make your partner's vulnerability about you. Allow yourself to step into their shoes for a minute even if you don't agree with what's being said.

3. **L.U.V.** **L**isten first, **U**nderstand second, and **V**alidate third. My clients probably think I sound like a broken record with this one but this is a key component to rebuilding the connection between you and your partner. When you're actively listening to understand, you begin to learn more about your partner's wants and needs through empathy. If you feel like you're not fully understanding what your partner is attempting to convey, don't hesitate to ask questions to gain clarity. And last but not least, validate your partner's feelings. This is simply allowing your partner to have a specific point of view even if you do not agree.

So, we've done some unpacking and we've also discussed some tips for handling your partner's truth. Now let's dive into that pesky little thing called pride.

# Set Aside Your Pride

I've witnessed pride kill more intimacy than the Grim Reaper. I use this personification of death because self-centered pride diminishes, devalues, and ultimately destroys intimacy. But let's rewind a bit and define the word pride in and of itself. Pride, according to the Merriam-Webster Dictionary, is defined as the quality or state of being proud such as a reasonable self-esteem; confidence and satisfaction in oneself, pleasure that comes from some relationship, association, achievement, or possession that is seen as a source of honor, respect, etc.

Authentic pride typically has a positive connotation and descriptors that include words like "accomplishment", "mastery", "triumph", "confidence" and "self-worth". It is positively associated with self-esteem and negatively associated with shame-proneness[4]. In my time of working with couples, I've seen how egotistically prideful behavior leads to a sense of entitlement and superiority amongst one another. When one or both people in a relationship significantly holds their pride hostage, the focus becomes more about pointing out each other's flaws, blame-shifting, invalidating one another, lack of accountability, domination, and/or an unwillingness to compromise.

Many times, one or both partners tend to feel they are right and their partner is wrong. They may even say, "okay, I know I have my faults, but they do this or that". Now it becomes a competition and intimacy begins to fade in the process.

So, how exactly can pride show up in a relationship? First, you lack gratitude. You don't acknowledge the positive or helpful things your partner does and you take them for granted. Second, you don't respectfully ask for things. You either just take, state orders, or make demands. Third, you typically ignore your partner's requests or desires. And fourth, you never feel that you are wrong or admit to any wrongdoing.

**Let's Unpack:**

1. Have you been showing up as prideful in your relationship with your partner according to the key points listed above?

2. Why have you been so prideful? Are you embarrassed or ashamed of something and those feelings tend to be exhibited in your behavior?

3. Do you feel that you're always right and your partner is wrong because you actually have a poor sense of self-worth?

4. Do you feel that you are above correction or constructive criticism?

5. Have you felt taken advantage of by your partner for quite some time and instead of using effective communication strategies and creating boundaries, you allow pride to do the talking?

I know, this is another gut punch but again, this is a safe space. Be honest with yourself regarding the areas that are challenging for you to recognize. Allow yourself to reflect over these questions until you begin to get to the root of your pride.

# Closer Than Close

With all this talk about vulnerability, embracing each other's truth, and putting pride in its proper place, let's dive into reconnecting and rebuilding emotional intimacy. When emotional intimacy has plummeted, typically it's because of unresolved hurts, resentment, conflicts, or feeling unsafe to be vulnerable in a relationship. Let's discuss some ways in which you can become closer to each other; one step at a time.

### Tips for regaining closeness and connection in your relationship:

1. **Check yourself.** It's very easy to assume that we have no faults or that our faults are miniscule in comparison to our partner's. Be willing to take ownership of your actions. Even if it's just being distracted by other things when your partner is trying to communicate with you. Take accountability for that.

2. **Periodic check-ins.** Ask your partner from time to time if there's anything they desire from you as opposed to waiting for your partner to initiate that conversation all the time. This shows your partner that you care and that they are more than an afterthought to you. Don't allow anything or anyone else to consistently take priority over your partner.

3. **Don't Avoid Tough Conversations.** I know this isn't always easy, especially if there's been a history of your partner becoming upset or distant when you try to approach certain conversations, but it's important that persistent issues are

being addressed so that they do not fester. In the next chapter, I will be discussing how to resolve conflict with love.

4. **Compliment and Appreciate Your Partner More.** I know this seems self-explanatory, but it's important that I remind you that a nice gesture goes a long way. Remember, being in a relationship is a choice and if the two of you are choosing to be there, a little acknowledgment can turn a distant relationship into a close one.

5. **Maintain Physical Intimacy.** This does not always mean sexual intercourse, even though that's one aspect of it. But be sure to give your partner a loving hug or kiss, rub their back or feet sometimes, hold their hand, try giving them a massage, or even wash their body in the shower or bathtub. Various studies have found that couples who touch each other tend to be happier and more satisfied in their relationships. Studies also show that repeated positive touch tends to be linked to increased oxytocin. But again, you have to create a safe space for your partner so that this becomes more of a natural occurrence.

Hopefully, you are taking mental notes and will attempt to apply these strategies together. It's important to remember that both of you have to be willing participants in this process in order to see results. If you are having difficulty with any one of these tips, go back to the drawing board and ask yourself why. Always do your best to first identify the root causes of your challenges so that you can effectively communicate them to each other. Be willing to listen with an open mind and remember, you are not opponents. You are on the same team.

# WHEN IT HURTS

## Resolving Conflict With Love

---

*"Conflict can and should be handled constructively; when it is, relationships benefit. Conflict avoidance is \*not\* the hallmark of a good relationship. On the contrary, it is a symptom of serious problems and of poor communication."*

HARRIET B. BRAIKER
Psychologist, Author, and Expert on Women's Issues

*"If you talk to a man in a language he understands, that goes to his head. If you talk to him in his language, that goes to his heart."*

NELSON MANDELA
South African Anti-Apartheid Revolutionary
and Political Leader

Let's keep it all the way real for a moment. What bothers you the most; the message your partner delivers to you in a conflict or their actual delivery of the message? If we're honest, it's probably both but many times, it's how a message is conveyed that determines the direction in which a conflict may go. I'm pretty sure you've heard the quote, "*10% of conflict is due to difference of opinion and 90% is due to delivery and tone of voice.*" I have found this to be true in many instances with my clients.

I've been called everything from the "wife-whisperer" to the "logical queen" and even the "erotic missionary" due to how I convey messages to my clients. I actually find these nicknames kind of cute but I also understand why they have been given to me. Many times my clients will say, "Angie, you're literally saying the same thing I say to my partner all the time. Why can't they receive it from me like they receive it from you?" The reason for this is because typically when someone is speaking to me, I'm applying the acronym L.U.V. which I stated in the previous chapter (Listening, Understanding, and Validating), but I'm also applying the Three Ts: Timing, Tone, and Tact. Whenever I'm communicating with someone, especially when there's conflict or a potential conflict, my goal is to speak to the person in *their* language, not mine. This doesn't mean that I dilute the message. It just means that I speak to them in a way they can best receive what I'm saying and this is something you can simply apply as well.

# The Three Ts: Timing, Tone, & Tact

When it comes to conflict, specifically with your partner, always keep your overall goal in mind. If your goal is to one up your partner, make them look and feel bad, prove a point, or maintain the champion title of who can act an entire fool the longest, then the Three Ts will not apply to you. But if your goal is to understand one another, honor each other's voice, and ultimately reconnect and resolve conflict, then you're still in the right place. So let's begin, shall we?

The first "T" is timing. There are so many times a conflict could have been resolved if we considered the timing in which we approached the conflict. Say for instance, your partner had a huge blowout with a close family member or friend but you want to discuss why the both of you haven't had a date night since the movie *Love Jones* premiered. Okay, so I'm exaggerating a little bit, but basically it's been a really long time since the both of you have intentionally spent some quality time together. Considering how well you know your partner, ask yourself if addressing the issue is the right time. If you truly believe the answer is no, I want you to make a mental note to bring it up at a later date or express to your partner that you would like to discuss a topic that's been on your mind but at a more appropriate time. Again, the focus is on timing. I'm not encouraging you to forgo your wants and desires, but table it for another time (not a perfect time, because usually that doesn't exist) you think your partner may be able to be open to discussing the issue with a level head.

The second "T" is tone. When we say "watch your tone", this doesn't just apply to children. This can be relevant to adults as well. Raise your hand if you've been told once or twice that you have a "slick mouth" or you're something like a "Petty Betty' or maybe you're known for hitting below the belt. If this sounds like you, checking your tone may be a bit more challenging but it can still be accomplished. We all know that you can literally say the same statement in a multitude of ways and they take on different meanings. In order to resolve conflict with love, this is something you will have to practice quite frequently until you get the hang of it. And feel free to practice with a friend who will provide you with honest feedback on how you say things. We can't expect our partners to respond favorably to us when we choose to not be aware and take responsibility for our tone.

The third "T" is tact. Being tactful also has its place when it comes to conveying a message. This is where my clients tend to get a bit stumped because they may feel like they are sugarcoating the message or "walking on eggshells" with their partner which leads them to feeling inauthentic. So here's a key takeaway. Utilize tactfulness when dealing with more sensitive topics such as sexual pleasure, your partner's weight, or anything you have noticed to be a bit more difficult for your partner to digest.

Everyone is not the same so what may bother your partner, may not bother you. But also remember, you have a bit of a sore spot for certain things as well that you would also appreciate your partner handling with care. So, apply that same thoughtfulness and understanding towards your partner when addressing certain topics. And if you are still unsure of what wording to use, try looking up some synonyms of the words you are trying to express. Think about it this way, telling your partner that you're unhappy in your relationship may hurt but if you say, "I've been feeling a bit down about some things concerning our relationship", this is a more tactful way to state your concerns. This also allows for you and your partner to have dialogue and understand each other as opposed to your partner feeling like they are responsible for your overall unhappiness.

# I Have Something To Say

I'm no stranger to using communication strategies with adults that I've used with children as well. Remember when I mentioned earlier about how our first experiences with intimacy in childhood and adolescence pretty much shapes how we interact in romantic relationships? Well, another thing I've noticed is that when children are taught early on how to communicate their needs and wants effectively, this can also follow them into adulthood.

Thomas Gordon was an American clinical psychologist widely recognized as a pioneer in teaching communication skills and conflict resolution methods to parents and teachers. One of his most commonly used strategies includes the I-message. When I was a school social worker, I taught students from pre-kindergarten to twelfth grade about the I-message and how it could be a game changer in their communication skills. I later began to integrate this same strategy while working with couples.

The I-message focuses on three parts: (1) Behavior: What is happening around you and what the person is doing, (2) Feeling: How does the person's behavior make you feel, and (3) Consequence: What happens as a result.

**Let's Unpack:**

1. When approaching a conflict with your partner, try to get as clear as possible on what's going on or what your partner is doing. This is the first part in utilizing an I-message which is identifying the undesirable behavior. The more clear you are, the better you can effectively communicate what is specifically bothering you.

2. Identify your specific feelings surrounding the undesired behavior (i.e. I feel frustrated, I feel taken advantage of, I feel left out, I feel unloved, I feel dismissed etc.). Remember, these are YOUR feelings, not your partner's. But your feelings are still valid, even if they do not agree.

3. Many times when we think of consequences, we associate it with something negative or some form of punishment. But I want you to view the consequence as something you would like to see as a result of you sharing your feelings (i.e. I would like you to use respectful words towards me as opposed to calling me out of my name or making fun of me). Be sure to be confident, clear, and concise in your request.

I.message example: *"When you tell me that I sound stupid for sharing my feelings with you, I feel dismissed and disrespected. I would really like for you to validate my feelings, even when you don't agree."*

As always, this is a two-way street. When one partner shares their truth in the form of an I-message, they are expressing their vulnerability so it's up to the other partner to be able to handle their truth and create a safe space for their voice to be heard. You'll see how all of these skills tend to build upon one another to reignite passion, pleasure, and connection in your relationship.

# Effective Conflict Resolution

Now that we've discussed the Three Ts and the I-message, we can tie all of this together by practicing effective conflict resolution. It's important to be aware of how you deliver a message as well as being clear on what your partner is doing that upsets you in order to approach this last step. It can be quite challenging to resolve conflict if we have not practiced those skills first.

**Steps for effectively resolving conflict:**

1. Set aside some uninterrupted time for the both of you to resolve the conflict, preferably at least 30 minutes. Decide on the meeting place, date, and time and don't forget to have pen and paper or your phone to jot down notes.

2. Think of one specific problem you would like to resolve (i.e. how we become verbally disrespectful to one another when we're hurting, or some kind of unfairness or inequality when it comes to performing household chores). Remember to be as specific as possible.

3. Without blaming each other, list the things you've personally done that haven't helped to resolve the problem. This allows for both partners to take accountability for the conflict. A conflict typically involves two or more people, even if it's the enabler.

4. List at least three to five possible solutions for solving the problem and do not judge the solutions. Just allow yourself to think of various ways to solve the problem, even if you do not

agree. This is just a brainstorming technique and will be evaluated later.

5. Now, list the advantages and disadvantages of each solution. Try your best to be as objective as possible and rate each solution on a scale from 0-5, 0 being not useful at all and 5 being very useful.

6. Try your best to align the solutions and see which ones you both can agree on. If this is your first time practicing conflict resolution, use this as a trial period to see what works. You can always come back and tweak or change anything that's not beneficial.

7. Plan and agree how you will each carry out the chosen solutions and again, be as specific as possible to avoid confusion.

8. List possible barriers that may hinder your success during implementation and decide how to overcome them.

9. Follow up by scheduling the time, date, and the meeting place to discuss progress. Try to give yourselves about a week before meeting again. If there are some hiccups, try not to get discouraged. Just be willing to try again as a couple and start from the beginning.

10. Pay attention to one another and recognize each other's efforts. Provide positive feedback and try establishing check-ins on a consistent basis.

So, I know that was a lot and if we're honest, talking about conflict resolution is not exactly the sexiest topic. But when done with a willingness and openness, it can truly aid a couple in feeling more connected, which is the goal.

## THE SPICE OF LIFE

# Strengthening Your Physical Intimacy & Sexual Passion

---

*"To feel aroused is to feel alive."*

FIONA THRUST
Erotica Writer

*"Sexual energy comes into play before sex even takes place. The greatest pleasure isn't sex, but the passion with which it is practiced."*

PAULO COELHO
Brazilian Lyricist and Novelist

So, for many of you who saw the words, *Passion* and *Pleasure* in the title of my book and were thinking, "Yes! I'm ready to learn some new tricks and spice up my relationship or marriage", this part will definitely tickle your fancy, but in a more detailed and thorough way. My goal is to help you peel back the layers so you can truly understand how to connect with your partner on a physical level. But here's the caveat; it begins with YOU.

# Are You Living or Just Existing?

You've probably heard the phrase, "Are you living or just existing?" with regards to various situations. But, have you ever heard it in the context of passion and pleasure in your relationship? When I'm working with couples and they express their frustrations in terms of boring and disconnected sex, or experiencing "let's just get it over with sex", I often try to get them to understand that if they are not even showing up for themselves in an exciting way, then it's kind of hard to expect that from their partners.

The harsh truth is that many people are just going through the motions. They get up in the morning, mindlessly groom themselves (i.e. shower/bathe, brush their teeth, wash their faces, brush or style their hair, maybe even take it a step further and moisturize their skin and dab a little makeup), maybe quickly fix and eat breakfast or order something on the way to work, listen to the same radio station in the car, enter the office, do the same work and often complain about it, hop back in the car, head home, either fuss and complain with their partner or the complete opposite which is to not say two words to one another, allow the kids to practically be raised by their tablets or iPads, disengage from everyone in the house, thoughtlessly scroll on social media, eat a mediocre meal, and then head to bed just to get up and do the same thing all over again. Now I don't know about you, but what can you honestly say about this that screams purpose, fulfilling your dreams, being grateful, embracing change and growth, enjoying the present moment, excitement, or freedom?

I know you're wondering how all of this connects to passion and pleasure so I'll break it down for you. If you woke up this morning and you're still here, then it's apparent that you are alive. But if you're not exactly connected to your emotions or feelings, or you often feel that pretty much everything is outside of your control, or things are always happening *to* you, then you are merely existing. This can actually feel like you're dying a slow death void of joy, happiness, and passion. But when you're living, you're open to the world around you, you do things that you love and enjoy, you allow yourself to engage in relationships that fulfill you, you don't get too caught up in false expectations about how you should be, and you take responsibility for your life. This is where passion and pleasure emerges and tends to be reflected in physical intimacy as well.

## Tips for living and not just existing:

1. **Be vulnerable.** Don't be afraid to ask yourself hard questions, dig deeper, and make self-discovery a priority.

2. **Do what you like.** Become more comfortable doing what you want to do as opposed to doing what you feel is expected of you. You have to dictate your life, otherwise, you'll find yourself living out someone else's dreams and goals which tends to lead to dissatisfaction, resentment, and unfulfillment.

3. **Be grateful for the little things.** When you allow yourself to appreciate that close parking space you scored at the grocery store, or the jeans that were a little snug last year but now fits just right, or that extra seven dollars you didn't know you had on your Starbucks gift card, you start becoming more aware of things to be grateful for and you won't take anything for granted.

4. **Stop seeking approval.** Know that you are more than enough and that confidence comes from within. This builds assuredness and helps you to not second guess yourself so often.

5. **Stop escaping.** Instead of drowning yourself in menial tasks or allowing yourself to become distracted by any and everything

instead of facing issues head on, create a life that you don't feel like you have to escape from.

6. **Find purpose.** Find things that motivate you and make life worth living.

7. **Control what you can and release the rest.** There are plenty of things you can control in your life (i.e. how you choose to respond, what you give your attention to, your reaction, etc.) and then there are things that you just have absolutely no control over (i.e, the weather, the managerial structure at your job, or people's responses to things, etc). Don't spend another moment stirring over what's uncontrollable. Choose freedom.

# Indulge the Senses

For many of us, we learned about the five senses in preschool or elementary school. I even remember the old school flashcards with a picture of a mouth with a tongue sticking out indicating the sense of taste, or a picture of an ear to indicate the sense of hearing, along with a hand for touch, eyes to see, and a nose to smell. Seems very basic, right? Little did we know at the tender ages of four and five how much would be guided by our senses. We use our senses to gather and respond to information about our environment, which aids in our survival. Each sense provides different information which is combined and interpreted by our brain[5].

When we think of passion and pleasure, the senses play a significant role in our responses. What we see, smell, touch, hear, and taste can either heighten or diminish our sexual arousal. Without going too deep into a lesson on the sexual response cycle, the four basic phases include: excitement, plateau, orgasm, and resolution. For the purposes of this section of the book, we're going to focus on excitement and learning how to get there before sex even begins.

During the sexual response cycle, excitement may include an increase in muscle tension, accelerated breathing, nipples becoming hardened or erect, increased blood flow to the genitals, vaginal lubrication, breasts becoming fuller, or swelling of the testicles. I know you get the point. We're all adults here. But in certain instances, if passion and pleasure has dwindled in a relationship, how can you even get to this first phase of excitement? Let's take a look at how indulging in the senses can help with this.

Every sexual experience starts in your senses. Whether it's a touch, a taste, a scent, a sound or sight, arousal starts in the brain.

Often it happens long before you even consciously think about having sex. Your five senses bring in an extraordinary amount of primal information in a split second[6]. Awareness is what allows you to be in the present moment and curate your experiences so that you may enjoy sex to the fullest.

## Tips for indulging in the senses to produce better physical intimacy:

1. **Slow down.** In Western culture, we are truly a fast-paced society. Everything from scarfing down our food without even taking a minute to breathe to not taking adequate time off work to cope with life transitions, we're always on the go. Slowing down and being present can assist with enjoying moments with our partner such as cuddling and caressing each other while watching a movie or taking our time to build up our physiological responses to sex. This is a mindfulness practice that allows us to absorb what we're feeling in the moment. Also, one of the first stepping stones to increasing pleasure.

2. **Explore what you like.** This may include some solo sessions of self-pleasure or just even taking time to figure out what hobbies you enjoy. This could be anything from painting to fishing but be sure to explore the things that allow you to feel present and alive. Trust me, when you begin participating in healthy leisure on a consistent basis, you're more inclined to bring that same energy into the bedroom.

3. *Try to indulge in one or more of your senses daily.* This could look like basking in the sunlight that peeps through your window in the morning, relishing the smell of a great cup of coffee, taking your time and savoring a delicious meal, allowing yourself to delight in one of your favorite songs, or taking pleasure in the feeling of warm, clean sheets after a relaxing shower or bath.

Then, translate that same indulgence in the bedroom such as appreciating the sight of your partner's body, enjoying the smell of their natural scent, taking pleasure in your partner's touch on your skin and the sounds they make during lovemaking, and delighting in the taste of their essence.

Being keenly aware of your senses can definitely magnify your physical intimacy, but it requires you to be present. Do yourself a favor and slow down. Pay more attention to what pleases you in *and* outside of the bedroom. Take inventory and be open and willing to share this with your partner.

# Become a Student of Your Partner

I find it rather intriguing that we are willing to put so much energy towards learning the necessary skills to perform well at our jobs, or trying to meet our children's every need, or even staying abreast of pop culture and the latest gadgets like our life depends on it, but we don't put that same effort into studying our partners. We will never be mind readers of one another, so that shouldn't be expected, but we can find more ways to be more in tune with each other just by observing, asking questions, and trying new things.

Becoming a student of your partner can definitely exhibit a high level of care. When you make the effort to learn more about each other's turn ons and turn offs, you're essentially saying to your partner that they are a priority to you. If you recall the initial dating stage, there were probably lots of questions, conversations, and a willingness to explore one another. This is more than likely attributed to the newness of your relationship and the excitement of the unknown. With time, we know that the novelty tends to fade, we become complacent even though we're always evolving, and the passion and pleasure tends to take a back seat. But no matter how long you've been with your partner, you should never stop learning. If you want your physical intimacy to thrive, you have to be willing to adapt to the evolution of your partner.

Something I've observed in relationships that doesn't quite get discussed enough is consent. Many times, we think that because we've been in a long-term relationship with someone, our partners should just be accustomed to how we initiate and perform sexual acts. Consent boils down to three things: questions, respect, and trust. Many times, this is lost or even ignored in long-term relationships because we assume that we know everything about our partners.

Consent not only applies to women, but to men as well. If we're honest, many people did not exactly grow up with the healthiest experiences and views of sex, so ensuring that your sexual encounters with one another is always consensual, is not only thoughtful but it can be quite sexy as well. When you feel that you have autonomy over your body, this can lead to more confidence and better sexual experiences.

With reference to the previous section regarding indulging the senses, this is absolutely a great place to start. When you can create an atmosphere around what your partner essentially enjoys, you can actually be a few steps ahead of the game. If your partner enjoys visual stimulation, wearing certain clothing may be a huge turn on for them. And as always, if you're unsure, you can ask what they would like to see you wear. If your partner is a sucker for aromas and scents, you can adorn your home with scented candles or incense to create a mood that instantly excites or arouses them. If your partner is a foodie, cooking a delightful meal or treating them to a restaurant that they enjoy can also be a winner. The main thing is to study your partner and referring to the senses can be a great starting point.

When prioritizing your partner's sexual pleasure, praise your partner for enjoying themselves. What I mean by that is sometimes we aren't always given permission to feel pleasure. As a matter of fact, many messages in society surrounding pleasure focus on diminishing yourself in order to make others feel good. But for the sake of studying your partner, we're going to flip that and allow your partner to release any guilt regarding what they enjoy. If you're caressing your partner and they let out a light moan, tell them how much you love to see them enjoying themselves. You can also ask them if they would like for you to continue. This gives your partner the opportunity to provide consent and enjoy themselves all in one.

**Tips for studying your partner:**

1. ***Prioritize.*** As the saying goes, "energy flows where attention goes", so be more intentional about focusing on what your partner desires. The nuances, their mannerisms, and body language are just a few things that can help guide you when studying your partner.

2. ***Take notes.*** Even if you have to write down your partner's specific desires or special occasion dates so that you don't forget, be sure to do that!

3. ***Ask questions.*** When in doubt, just ask. Try your best to never assume. Now there will be times your partner just wants you to "know" things, but the only way to know is to ask. Be in the present moment with your partner when they are sharing their thoughts and feelings. Try not to zone out or preoccupy yourself with other things.

4. ***Make time.*** In order to improve your physical intimacy, you have to make time to connect in that way. It's so easy to lose focus on physical connection due to daily distractions, but be sure to make time for hugs, kisses, cuddling, massages, and sex. None of this stuff is going to just happen on its own so make the time.

5. ***Solicit feedback.*** Ask your partner with an open mind if what you're doing for them excites them. But be ready to receive constructive criticism as well. This is a sure fire way to learn if you're on the right track or if adjustments are needed.

6. ***Never stop learning.*** This is where many couples drop the ball, hence why this book was created. The moment you stop learning your partner, is the moment intimacy begins to fade. Learn about your partner's physical needs and changes so that you can grow with them. This can include everything from

pregnancy, to erectile dysfunction, to menopause. Don't be stagnant thinking that what you were doing in year one of your relationship will apply in year ten. Just like we're always evolving as people, our bodies are evolving as well and it may require a different kind of loving to keep the spark alive.

Reigniting passion, pleasure, and connection in your relationship is definitely a joint effort that takes practice. I specify this because if you believe that reading this book one time without application will magically solve all of your intimacy problems, then there's still work to be done. But if you and your partner become intentional about what you've just read and begin to prioritize one another in this way, you will witness a beautiful and more harmonious intimate relationship emerge. When couples seek to learn about one another, they are essentially learning about themselves. This book is not intended to encourage perfection, but a willingness to try and provide each other with grace. Again, intimacy is about closeness so creating an environment within your relationship that embraces that closeness will produce the passion, pleasure, and connection you desire.

# Notes

My husband and I separated in year nine of our marriage. Our children were 4 and 9 years old at the time and I remember feeling an overwhelming sense of confusion, and just complete sadness. I couldn't understand what went wrong. I just knew that I couldn't continue on in my marriage and I felt the longer we stayed together, things would get worse. I didn't exactly know what worse would look like, but I didn't want to take the chance in subjecting our children to parents who were constantly at odds, disconnected and couldn't get along. So in my mind, I thought divorcing would be the lesser of two evils.

I desired a level of emotional intimacy in my marriage that I didn't know how to express because I feared my husband wouldn't understand what I was asking for, thus leading him to feel angry or even inadequate because in a sense, I was exhibiting a level of unhappiness that he was unable to fix. I was stuck because I would often think to myself, *"Angie, get a grip. Your husband comes home faithfully at night, he has a strong work ethic and always pays the bills on time, he definitely doesn't abuse you so saying you want a divorce is going to sound absolutely absurd and other people are going to think you're crazy as well."* But I wanted my husband to know all of me and not just in the context of me being his wife and mother of his children. I essentially wanted more than a provider and protector, but I didn't know why nor did I know how to communicate that to him.

In modern society, relationships and marriage look rather different in comparison to thirty plus years ago. Previously, survival and security tended to be the goal when it came to marriage so focusing on feelings and connectedness was not exactly a top priority. Yes, it may have been considered but not at the expense of breaking up a family. But now in modern society, we have a renewed sense of self (and sometimes inflated, if we're honest), we're learning more about ourselves and our thought processes at a rapid pace, and quite honestly, we have more distractions and things pulling us away from growing together in a relationship. As connected as we are through technology, we're not exactly "close" as a society.

There were times my husband and I attempted to connect on a deeper level, but I would often say it felt like we were in two different hemispheres because it seemed like we were in different climates speaking different languages. That's how distant I felt from him. We were lost in the sense that we both wanted to feel understood and desired, but we didn't know what to do about it. We attempted couples counseling but the one time we attended a session, it felt like an epic fail because the counselor took one look at us and concluded that we really didn't have any issues since we didn't come in the door kicking and screaming. I remember being so frustrated after that session because I'd often wondered where's the help for couples who may not exactly "look" like something is wrong, but something is seriously wrong.

We were just winging it many times in our marriage like a lot of couples do. We just took things day by day and figured whatever cards we were dealt, then we would go from there. At the beginning of a relationship, you find yourself attracted to someone, you're excited just to talk to them, you begin spending much more time together, you realize you have some common interests and goals, and then boom, you're locked in. But no one teaches you that in order to have a close and healthy relationship, you have to be willing to understand your partner's perspective, how to essentially "fight fair" because disagreements will ensue, how to be on one accord with regards to specific obligations, and how to really understand what physical intimacy does to and for a relationship.

Thankfully, our separation did us a world of good, but it was still very hard to navigate because we had to really pinpoint what caused our closeness to drift. That meant we had to take a hard look at ourselves individually first and do the necessary work to rebuild our relationship. Due to us separating, we were somewhat forced to have harder conversations with one another, be more transparent about what we felt we wanted and needed, but also take accountability for the breakdown of our relationship.

Now, after eighteen years of marriage, we can truly understand where things went south for us back then and because of those same skills we learned, we're able to still apply it today and bounce back a lot quicker in order to maintain the closeness in our marriage. Sustaining a healthy and close relationship in modern society for sure comes with its challenges and it takes a lot more than just saying you want an intimate relationship. It requires a willingness to learn and grow with one another, but also an overall desire to really know and embrace each other.

There was a time when my husband and I were looking at signed divorce papers on our kitchen counter and now I look up and see the position I'm in today as an intimacy coach. At that time, I could not have predicted this is what I would be doing. But it all makes sense now and I feel blessed and honored to be able to share my personal as well as professional experiences to help couples regain the passion, pleasure, and connection they desire in their relationships. It is my hope that this book has provided you with a different perspective, a deeper understanding along with specific skills that you can apply to your own intimate relationship, and a sense of excitement towards reinvigorating your relationship.

I want to thank my husband for being who he is and for allowing me to see more of him throughout the years so that I may better understand him. This in turn, has helped me to feel more comfortable and confident in showing up as my authentic self with him. I appreciate his vulnerability and willingness to share his most intimate thoughts with me. I value his presence in my life. I honor the safe space we have cultivated with one another and I look forward to many more years of exploring the depths of our relationship with love.

# Credits

1. "Vulnerability allows for people to understand each other on a deeper level, including their insecurities and their deepest feelings, which can lead to greater empathy in both partners," says Laura Sgro, a licensed psychotherapist from Los Angeles, California.

2. Family is the primary agent of socialization during childhood and, even in adolescence, it continues to be more influential than any other single factor. (Simons, Simons & Wallace, 2004).

3. Over time, experiences in the family of origin, particularly the quality of the parent-child relationship, have a major impact upon subsequent patterns of interaction with adult romantic partners through their impact on youth's acquisition of characteristics important to intimate relationships success. (Bryant, 2006; Conger, Cui, Bryant & Elder, 2000).

4. Brown, Brené. *Atlas of the Heart*, Random House, 2021.

5. Our senses are so important in that it allows us to gather information about our environment, which aids in our survival. Each sense provides different information which is combined and interpreted by our brain. "The Senses Working Together" https://tinyurl.com/4ccuyhwf. 5 September 2018.

6. Every sexual experience starts in your senses. Whether it's a touch, a taste, a scent, a sound or sight, arousal starts in the brain. Often it happens long before you even consciously think about having sex. Your five senses bring in an extraordinary amount of primal information in a split second. "Good Sex Starts In Your Senses" https://tinyurl.com/2h77czny. 6 July 2023.

www.ingramcontent.com/pod-product-compliance
Lightning Source LLC
Chambersburg PA
CBHW030536080526
44585CB00014B/964